My Life in Pictures

MY LIFE IN PICTURES

Poems

CHRISTIAN MCPHERSON

N_1 O_2 N_1
CANADA

Library and Archives Canada Cataloguing in Publication

McPherson, Christian
My life in pictures / Christian McPherson.

Poems.
ISBN 978-1-926942-15-5

I. Title.

PS8625.P53M9 2013   C811'.6   C2012-907977-4

Printed and bound in Canada on 100% recycled paper.

Now Or Never Publishing
#1101, 1003 Pacific Street
Vancouver, British Columbia
Canada V6E 4P2

nonpublishing.com
Fighting Words.

For my ~~step~~brother, Graham O'Neil
who watched many of these movies with me
all my love

The following feature is not intended for children.
It contains scenes of violence, coarse language and nudity.
Some adults may be offended by the content.
Viewer discretion is advised.

Based on a true story.

TAKE ONE

EASY RIDER (1969)

Sitting in my friend's room
we are 15-year-old boys
(pimpled, masturbating at home four times daily)
the weight of the world
about to ooze its gravity
upon us in heaps
yes
the discovery of things almost
adult

> difficult bra latches
> vomiting beer in the medicine dens
> > of hapless welfare stooges
> having to sit down
> > from inhaling too deeply
> jumping off garage rooftops
> > like ninjas
> > like Remo Williams
> watching the clouds turn into witches
> > and stir the cauldron of the moon

"listen to this" he says
pulling a Jimi Hendrix record
from its purple haze sleeve

yes
this was the moment where things changed
this was the moment where adulthood slaughtered us
it was in those notes

they took us to a magic land
psychedelic blues blistered our ears
and our jaws bounced along the floor
thumping away

a John Bonham drum solo came next
and Jim Morrison crucified
any teddy bear leftovers that might
have been hanging around

yes
in a few years I would come to the conclusion
while listening to Madonna and Boy George
squealing synthesized popularity over the radio
that I was most definitely born
in the wrong time
that I should have been born in the sixties

did you see Dennis Hopper and Peter Fonda?
I mean they were so cool it hurt
my little acid fuelled brain

and Jack in his football helmet
looking like a nutbar
gearing up for his role in Cuckoo's Nest
          I couldn't take my eyes off of him

I had fallen in love
with a people
with a time
with a lifestyle

I had fallen in love
with a fashion
with a music
with a film
          that wasn't mine
                    I was an ex-pat of the present

I reluctantly came out of my mother's womb
at the end of August 1970

if you do the math
my father juiced my mother
in the last months of 1969
my conception
a wiggly sperm foothold on the sixties

I was indeed an Easy Rider.

Butch Cassidy and the Sundance Kid (1969)

In utero
in the cosy dark
of my mother's womb
maybe here is where
my love of cinema was born?
           (it almost always feels wet
                    when the lights dim)

now as an adult
in the grocery store
I reach for a bottle of
Newman's Own salad dressing
and think about his voice
and those blue eyes

I like to think that when
my mother was pregnant
that "Butch Cassidy
          and the Sundance Kid"
          was the first movie
I could be said to experience

I like to think a little piece
of William Goldman's
witty dialogue flew from
Newman's lips
          (really only a vibration
                    on a fetal pole)
                    and fused with my DNA

a writer was soon to be born

pupils dilate in the dim light
24 frames per second
      move
            Redford's moustache
            around on horseback
      only sexy to my mother
but I'm sure my father thought
cool
or so I like to think.

LOVE STORY (1970)

For me
there are no memories
just pictures

a faded Polaroid
I can imagine the sound
of my uncle pulling it
from the camera's guts
stretching plastic tissue
snapping it in the air
between thumb and forefinger
        thack thack thack thack
the black turning to dark green
then dissolving to a golden honey brown
the image revealing itself
exposure

there is
my mother in pink
looking like Jackie O
looking like the beautiful
women of that time looked
        she could have been
        a radiant cult member
        or
        a Woodstock hippie
                (not the clothes, just the hair)

and she is holding me
a swathed white bundle in the hospital
ready to take me home for the first time
and behind her is my father
looking like he just won the lottery
        a smile so big
                that it could stop traffic
and he is wearing Buddy Holly glasses
and a plaid jacket
and my god they both look so young
and my god they look so in love

yes, this is the picture I think about
sometimes
and think
        what if?

this is the picture I think about
sometimes
and think
        this is what it was
                before it fell apart.

Harold and Maude (1971)

Like Harold
my fascination with death
has always been
an ongoing autopsy
in the theatre of my mind

I thought of my father
as I dissected my grade nine
science frog
        it prevented me
        from being squeamish

I can picture
his amber hair
        fluttering in the wind
        driving down the dirt road
        where the farmer had found
        the tracks
        the tracks that went off the road

        if dead, call Red
                he'd joked with my mother

before he married her
before he worked for National Cash Register
he had a short stint as an embalmer

he'd insert tubes into the arteries of cadavers
draining their blood directly into the sink
replacing it with life-ever-after fluid

he'd paint their faces
comb their hair
glue their mouths shut

he'd dress them up like dolls

makeup for the role of a lifetime

he told me
the worst one
was the car of teenaged kids

they had gone off the road
in their convertible
their bodies ended up
rotten fruit
hanging in the trees

a farmer had found them
three weeks later
after baking in the hot summer sun

he said they were like Jell-O
swollen fat
overinflated
blow-up dolls

the smell indescribable

he couldn't fix these ones
he couldn't make them pretty

the caskets
for their funerals
closed.

THE GETAWAY (1972)

My father was so Steve McQueen
    so cool
    and my mother
    prettier than Ali MacGraw

    love like theirs
    gives your whole life backlighting
    colours it by Technicolor

and didn't Sam Peckinpah
    always give you that slow burn
    a kind of Hitchcockian itch
    hold the camera a little too long
    make you fidget in your seat
    make you hide downstairs

the build up
violence made sexual
and then the
           POW!
    of the explosive ending

who knew Peckinpah
would come
and guest direct
a few scenes
at my home?

THE HOLY MOUNTAIN (1973)

Film
has always been
what music is for other people
what reading is for other people
what running or golf is for other people

film
has always been
my Fantastic Planet
my Jesus Christ Superstar
my Magnum Force
my Holy Mountain

film
my family
Sisters I never had

The Sting
of film
came early in my Amarcord childhood
the Papillon
floating by Charlotte's Web
dancing in the light of the Paper Moon

it would remind me later
about
Scenes from a Marriage
Don't Look Now
The Crazies
        The Exorcist

                The Way We Were

it would carry me through
my American Graffiti youth
of high school
        (Battle for the Planet of the Apes)

it would carry me
into the university Paper Chase
and my Live and Let Die attitude
questioning everything
right down to The Last Detail
an existential High Plains Drifter
on the Mean Streets of Westworld

film
and me
will never have
The Long Goodbye

not that is
until
Death shows up
        Enter the Dragon
        The Wicker Man
        The Day of the Jackal
        My Name is Nobody

film
and me
locked together
hanging upside down
defusing the bomb

the LED counting down

then the Soylent Green
finale

film
always about
being
human
in the end.

A WOMAN UNDER THE INFLUENCE (1974)

My Danish grandmother
could be
so Mommie Dearest
so Wicked Witch of the West
turning her husband into
The Invisible Man
          oh shut up and mind your business

when my mother was a young girl
my grandmother would beat her
and her sister
with sticks
for nothing

and yet my grandmother was always
so Mary Poppins
so Glenda, Good Witch of the North
with me

my mother told me
her way of coping
was to imagine a room
a perfect beautiful room

she would go to that room
whenever the sticks came out

she recreated those rooms
for her dolls

when she became an adult
she made her whole house
perfect

I've never seen a cleaner
more perfect home than mine

my father gave me a spanking
for something I did
recreating his own
horror movie childhood

I don't remember it
apparently it hurt
and I cried

my mother told him
never again

he never did

and to this day
my mother's home
remains perfect.

Snow White and the Seven Dwarfs (1937–1975)
RE–RELEASE

My first film
in a theatre
which is now long gone
I sat with my mother
on the ground floor
in the back
under the overhead hanging balcony
       the coziness of watching a rainstorm
       from the safety of the front porch

I don't remember much of Sneezy, Doc
or the rest of the crew
I do remember the old lady
and the poison apple

I remember the dark

it was this dark that became so ever important
it became my friend, my sadness, my joy, my terror
the dark became my life

movies became my everything
my religion, my memories, my conversations, my morality
and all it happened in the dark

cinema
      my shy lover
           embarrassed
                she always insisted on lights out

and now my kids own this film on Blu Ray
and watch it in the day with the lights on.

Jaws (1975)

White walls of the tires
looking like life preservers
simulated wood panelling
across its belly
my parents' brown station wagon
       Hooper: That's a twenty footer.
       Quint: Twenty-five. Three tons of him.

a black speaker
hangs off the inside driver's window
my father's window
wire curling back like fishing line
to the post

we are at the drive-in
       I am five

squished
between the vinyl front seats
in the armrest slot

John Williams' score
rippling sound waves
oscillating tuba notes
      Bah–dum
           Bah–dum

     "Come on into the water!"

my mother covers my eyes
I pry at her fingers, her palm

here comes the screaming
and the thrashing
and the blood
and then
      the calm

this film bit me
      and left celluloid scars
           upon my childhood

what were my parents thinking?

imagine the poster
      shark head
           mouth agape
              fish fangs ready
                to eat the girl
                  swimming across
                    the top

imagine the joke poster
      same shark head
           same fish fangs
              but it's coming out
              of a toilet

imagine me
      at five
      not understanding

me in my grandmother's bathroom
      floral wallpaper the stuff of bad acid trips
      the fuzzy turquoise toilet cover
      and matching rug
           blue finger sponges on the ocean floor

I'm inspecting the water
at the bottom of the bowl
looking for ripples
listening for oscillating tuba notes
I give it a pre-flush
just to make sure
that when I dump
that a shark
won't
swallow
me
whole.

FAMILY PLOT (1976)

Hitch's last

you never forget your first

mine just happened to be a threesome
Rear Window, Vertigo, and me

I was thirteen

my buttery tryst
       in the painful seats the Mayfair theatre
       (my church
              second home
       my father had worked in it
       when he was in high school
       had the keys to lock up)

in the dark
you caught on with Jimmy Stewart
figured it out with him

Hitch put you out there on the ledge
                   got you dizzy
                            scared

and didn't you love it?
and couldn't you not look away?

when I was six
I would build couch cushion forts
and watch the Saturday afternoon
black and white horror classics
      brown umbilical wire
          snaking from the TV channel changer
          snaking from my cave
          connecting me to my Monster's milk
          suckling the glass tit terror

when Lugosi or Karloff
      ventured too close to my window
      I was one click away to safety
          to the Wide World of Sports

Hitch made sure
all the windows and doors
were boarded up
from the outside
      (Rod Taylor forgot the chimney)
the monsters inside with you.

SATURDAY NIGHT FEVER (1977)

In my den
hangs a framed
newspaper article
about my father

his boots and black turtleneck
scream seventies zeitgeist

the article is about
what a success he was
how his art gallery was picture perfect

he and my mother would spend
a whole evening re-hanging the store
I would dance to the Brothers Gibb
doing my best Travolta

I was a child happy
to be getting lost
in the forest of tree trunk legs
of the wine and cheese
art openings
          coming out
          into the glass plate clearing of grapes and brie

borrowed dialogue
          twisting pearls around an index finger
                    lipstick lips encasing teeth
                              cigarette smoke curling up
                                        like it came from the starting gun

my mother and father anointing the walls
with the bindi stickers of sold
steam coming off the CHARGEX machine

my father would later go out
to celebrate with the artist
they ordered beer
and steaks
the size of thick bibles

when they were finished
they ordered two more.

Close Encounters of the Third Kind (1977)

A man gone crazy with the mash
piling his potatoes into a mountain
on his plate

my mother
still doing the homemaker ballet of the fifties
apron tutus of hot meals always ready for her men
roast beef, peas, mashed taters
        "Don't play with your food, Chris"

I'm in the hallway in the middle of the night
when the strange lights appear
how long did I stare at the phantom illuminations out my window?
was I sleepwalking again? pissing
into plants
what am I doing standing in the hallway?
did I wet the bed again?

Dreyfuss, manic, building a mountain in his living room
my father, building his Art Galley, his business
into a mountain, manic in our kitchen

did my mother throw the mashed potato first?
did my father retaliate with cooked vegetables?
        forecasting light peas with scattered utensils

pick a different day and watch the orange juice
fly across the fuck-you breakfast table

there were different times
        lots good, several nasty
there were different foods
        some eaten, some thrown
there were different dishes smashed

"Come on hit me, I dare you!"
the physicality of them
      scared me
           hiding in my couch fort in the basement
      the struggling,
      slap, slap, smash, crash and fuck you
      and fuck you too

"Call the police, Chris!"
      "Call 911, your father is hurting me!"

      terror, the thumping foot stamps of my parents
      doing the pugilist waltz above my head

the gash over my father's eye
broken glasses
someone went through the glass door

here comes the flashing lights
descending upon our lawn

                          again

not UFOs
just the police.

Star Wars (1977)

In the Bayshore shopping mall
in the toy section of The Hudson's Bay Company
is where I discovered
the characters of the film immortalized in plastic
          action figures

after I dwarfed the enthusiasm of a cheerleader
my parents bought me
(and following much careful consideration
on my part)
Chewbacca

he came with a special gun
none of the others figures had
the bowcaster
          (8.7 on the Fonzarelli cool scale)

I sat at the water fountain
where I played with him
until it was time to go

back in the station wagon
I realized I'd lost the gun
we had to go back
          "No way kid"

I was told they would buy me another one
that the bowcaster wasn't worth anything

through the tears and protests
my father spun his game show question
if I were offered Chewie or a washing machine
which would I pick?

"Jesus Christ, Chris, no!"

today that washing machine would be in a landfill
and my figure in the package would be worth
            the joy of a child?
how about the same price
                as a new washing machine.

Superman (1978)

In preschool
I would only answer
to the name Shazam!

in kindergarten I wore
a Batman cape to school
for the whole year

and later
like the alien
I would leave my perfect
crystal world
        (banned from the living room
                no footprints on the carpet
                    allowed)
when my friend asked me over
to play with his Lego

a strange dirty planet
a few dishes left in the sink
magazines left on the dining room table
is that dust?
who lives like this?
        animals

I hated going outside
never saw dirt
Allergy Boy
        Captain Hives
a sickly child
        broke both my arms
        (failed the flexed arm hang
        every year)
glasses to correct
my lazy eye

I pretended to be the alien
but really
I was
just
Clark Kent.

Kramer vs. Kramer (1979)

I'm sure my parents saw this one
did my mother relate more to Hoffman
or Streep?
       or was it just a subtle reminder
             a cracked mirror

it was the same year we went to Denmark
my mother's homeland

she came to Canada as a young girl
could hardly speak the language
a five person immigrant family in
a one bedroom apartment

she wore funny homemade dresses
she wore her embarrassment

she met my father in the church choir
the first time he asked her out
he asked her out
Friday and Saturday nights

now there we were
the happy family
     life preservers under the seats
       riding the metaphor
     to Legoland
     to the land of Hans Christian Anderson
     to the land of open faced sandwiches
     to the land of hot dogs the length of garter snakes
     and ice cream cones that looked like they were made
     by Santa Claus

in Tivoli Gardens
    there is a roller coaster
    my father kept giving the man tickets
    we rode it again and again
    nonstop
    a dozen times
    until the tickets ran out

shortly after
    back in the land of double bread
    my parents' marriage was running out of tickets too.

The Muppet Movie (1979)

I don't want to give you the wrong impression
paint you the wrong picture
direct you to the wrong theatre

most of the time my childhood
was Kermit the Frog

I had enough Lego bricks to build
God's asshole
I had
a pet cat
a freezer full of ice cream
cable TV

my Danish grandfather
would pick me up
on Saturday mornings
walk me down
to Bank Street
take me to Britton's Smoke Shop
beside my father's art gallery
and let me pick out a comic book
or two
get me some candy

he was a kind man
he was nice to me

when the ambulance
picked him up
yellow like dog piss
jaundice from the cancer
that was shortly going to kill him
the attendants asked
      how long have you been this colour?
he replied
      oh, just a few months

he was funny
like Fozzie Bear.

THE BLACK STALLION (1979)

A black horse running along a beach
a young boy atop his powerful back

this might have been the first film
where I experienced cinematography
and when I think of cinematography
I think of how a picture looks
I think of big expansive shots
I think about the aesthetics of a picture
I think about the beauty of a picture

there was a joke shop
that I liked to visit downtown
when I was a kid

the place sold magic tricks
and fake vomit
and fake dog shit
and whoopee cushions
and I loved it

it was there that I spied
the white little statuette
that had a big cartoon head
like something out of Mad Magazine
a statuette of a woman
that read on the bottom
"World's #1 Mom"

I saved my allowance
and when I had enough
I went and got it
and gave it to my mother
for Mother's day

I saw the disappointment
wash across her face

she told me
thank you
it was very nice
but
please don't buy me
stuff like this
I would rather have a card
drawn by you

this is tacky junk
stuff the McPhersons would have

I knew what she meant
my grandparents collected
tons of tchotchkes
glass animals from Red Rose
a plastic bird that would drink
when you wet his nose

it didn't fit
into my mother's perfect room

my father hated
where he grew up
so I understood
still the hurt on my face
evident

it was a nice gesture
she reassured me
very sweet
but we have to say goodbye

she threw it in the trash

that day I learned about aesthetics
that day I learned about beauty
that day I learned about truth.

STAR TREK: THE MOTION PICTURE (1979)

My parents
were passionate people
artistic people
musical people
>   my father always turning up the treble
>   the wah-wah pedal at the ready

they loved large
fought large
said it like it

>   was

it was the Vulcan
I related to the most
then later Sherlock Holmes
too

logic was devoid of emotion
it was pure and clean
it was something
that was very stable
dependable
it would never lie
it would never leave me
and above all
it always made sense

people didn't like
this Star Trek movie
said it didn't have the fun
of the original TV series

even as a kid
I liked its serious tone
its very Vulcan tone

logic
it has never left me
it's still my bread and butter
it's my safe place

I'd always return to it

still do.

XANADU (1980)

There was an antique wooden desk
in our basement rec room
where I sat and cried

schoolwork was dissolving me
I had been put in a special program
given a remedial reading teacher

I couldn't spell
        words made no sense
        Mr. Spock and mathematics were my
        intellectual soothers

my parents said we could all go
to the movies
on a school night
to see goddess Olivia Newton-John
in a roller-skating musical odyssey
        (the groove on my Grease LP
            well worn
        I would dance with the seriousness of accounting
        and the joy of a banana split)

I don't remember the assignment
I remember
the hollering to finish
the get-it-done-or-we're-not-going threats
I remember trying

        I wasn't doing it right

I don't remember anything about the film

my parents got divorced
I failed grade four

Xanadu.

TAKE TWO

SCANNERS (1981)

Crazy people
muttering to themselves

I didn't catch this one
until I was a teenager

it turned me on to
Cronenberg
and a lifelong
contemplation about identity

at age eleven
I'd become
obsessive compulsive
doing things
over and over
until they felt right

I would touch all the buttons
on the phone
until the feeling
the compulsion
would subside
like hunger disappearing
with the consumption
of a cheeseburger

I would mutter
to myself
all the first names
of my extended family
my goldfish
my cat

I'd chant their names
over and over
in a kind of holy prayer
a meditative mantra
to protect them

if I said their names
repeatedly
            twenty names
            a hundred times an hour
they wouldn't die
God would protect them
from all harm

I watched Prince Charles
and Lady Di
marry on TV
while I paced about
my father's new house
reciting names

I was keeping
my world safe

my obsession
didn't last
for more than a year

after which
the world
resumed
falling apart.

Escape from New York (1981)

My father and I came in late
      our eyes readjusting to the dark again
      our butts recalculating the seats once more
we had been racing Snake Plissken style
from Mel Brooks'
      "The History of the World: Part 1"
and before that
      the Get Smart movie
           "The Nude Bomb"

our third movie that day
      my father and I inspecting the newspaper ads
          like decoders of secret war maps
          plotting the best routes, times
          making sure it wasn't Restricted

the theatre was the runt of the day's litter
      one of the many tiny boxes of the Vanier Cineplex
people few in the seats

the film was dark
      and scary
          and adult
             and I loved it
      Kurt Russell was so cool
      he was cyberpunk before cyberpunk
      a futuristic pirate saving the President
      from the trash and scum suckers of Manhattan
      (we could use Snake Plissken now)

when it was over
my father suggested we stick around
to watch the beginning
to watch what we missed

we stayed for the whole thing again

it was the greatest day of my childhood
four films!
I asked my father about it
years later

he had no recollection.

RAIDERS OF THE LOST ARK (1981)

My eyes as wide as Alfred Molina's
watching Harrison Ford
about to grab the glowing golden idol

his fingers washing in the air
like seaweed in rough waves
anticipating it
switching it for a bag a sand
and in a flash
      it's done
            in the clear

not so fast, Indy

then
better be fast, Indy
      the poison arrows
      the spears
      THE BOULDER!

I'm now sitting
with my five and a half
year old son
and I'm wondering if he is
too young for this
am I going to repeat my parents'
mistakes
      grabbing the treasure too soon

we get to the scene
in the market
the crowd clears
a man in black twirls a massive sword
in Bruce Lee style
Indy calmly reaches for his gun
and shoots him

      my son roars with laughter

I smile
and reach for the popcorn.

POLTERGEIST (1982)

Living in an apartment
with my mother (nice place except for the rats
     and the guys who did dope in the basement)

chickenpox   ,
     my Danish grandmother
        with old medicine
        from the old country
     smeared me in a floury paste
     to stop the itching
        I was a powdered jelly doughnut intersecting
           a pin cushion
        making Linda Blair proud

then much later
well again
bag packed
     waiting at the door
     my father's van pulls up
        a sexy sectional couch in the back
        8-track playing the Beach Boys
     he takes me to see a showing of "Halloween"
     with his new girlfriend
        (an ex-ballet dancer no less)

     the headbangers in the audience
        with Iron Maiden jackets
        girls with hair teased high to the heavens
        jeans as tight as hell
           tight as a peel on an orange
           (the monkeys hungry
               post sin-oh-maniac)

my father laughing
    finding me hiding in the cinema's bathroom
    come back in, Pal
    what, are you scared?
    yes, let's go back in
        and watch a beautiful woman
            be strangled in her car

    6 months of men coming through my bedroom window
        nightly ritual flashlight checks
    the fish tank lights would keep
        Michael Myers at bay

my father's next logical choice
was a film about a house ripped apart
by supernatural entities
    (didn't even need booze in mine
        just delusions of grandeur)

when we arrived
the theatre was already packed
we sat at the very top
    (needed the popcorn Sherpa)
    backs to the projection booth wall
I could hear the mechanical whirl of the projector
I could see the cigarette smoke
    a thick cloud of ghostly apparitions
    descending on the crowd of non-smokers
    below

    trick kitchen chairs
    what would she do to him on that couch?

open the door
        a portal to another dimension

my father fucking her
        in some joy-of-sex lotus position
                on the floor

a bathrobe quickly appeared
        along with a sweaty face
        along with a twenty dollar bill
                corner store bubble gum bribery

happy to be out of the house
into the Walt Disney sunshine

bury those memories
in my Narnia closet

better yet
chain and padlock them
in the Evil Dead monster box
and bury them
deep under the house.

Blade Runner (1982)

The future had Atari in it
and no sunlight
Mister Deckard slurped noodles
  in the rain
   wearing his Bogart trench coat

tell me only the good things about your
     mother
       wakes me for soft boiled eggs
pulling them out of boiling water
   (not with her bare hands)
  no longer a housewife
    nurse, single mother
  making sure a hot breakfast
    was in my belly
  then off to work
I groggily make my way to the VCR
to see what Elwy Yost classic I'd snared
or CBC late night treasure I'd caught
in my magnetic tape trap
  a film a day before school
  magic window
window to your soul
  a replicant test
  milky owl gaze

  the pyramid of an American dollar bill
  he only does eyes
  crush them into your skull
  crush them into your twelve year old brain

seeing is believing
  and here I was believing hard
  baptised in celluloid

worshiping at the snack bar
the body of Daryl Hannah compels me
racoon eyes
looking like a post-apocalyptic hooker
cartwheeling onto Harrison Ford's head
(every straight boy's fantasy)

Rutger Hauer smashing his face
through a brick wall
a psychotic clown
        putting a nail through his hand
        making even Jesus wince
        a dying machine in the rain
        dying like we all die

don't we all want just a little more life, fucker?

my friend asked me
after the movie
        "How do you know you just didn't arrive
                here
        a second ago
        and that all your memories
        are just implants?"

philosophical puzzles
        memory implants

did it really happen that way?
        or was I older
        strung out on hash
        standing outside a bank machine

when I answered
        "Does it make any difference?"

ANNIE (1982)

My mother was now dating
the doctor upstairs
who would one day become
my stepfather

he was a brilliant man
read two books a week
read two newspapers a day
read too much

he was coming out of his own
failed marriage

he had rheumatoid arthritis
his toes and fingers
            knobby knotted roots

he always had pain
and he popped Percocet cocktails
and chased them down
with wine
then whisky
smoked Winstons
maybe a joint too

loaded up
I'm sure this is when he wrote
his monthly column on drugs
or
love poems
to my mother

he had a daughter
five years younger
than me
I don't think he was very nice
to her
I don't think he liked women
all that much

he liked me
which wasn't fair to her
but what could I do

I was a boy
and played chess
and had an interest in computers
and it made his big brain
firework

she was little
loved Annie
and would ask him
on her weekend visits
to take her again
and again
and he did
a half dozen times

maybe because they both
had red hair
or maybe she felt
like an orphan
          abandoned
whatever the reason
she loved it

it was probably
one of the nicer things
he did for her

I'm sure he thought
Annie
       not this cunt
              again.

THE BEST LITTLE WHOREHOUSE IN TEXAS (1982)

My father liked to drive

he would say
let's go for a little cruise
and we would get into his
vehicle and just
drive

sometimes we would
end up by the airport
on a dirt road
and park by the fence
and watch the planes
land

he would often
drive down to the market
to gaze at the prostitutes

look at the legs on that one he'd say
look at the shank on her
hey hey, pal
      pay attention
      check out the tits on that
              little darling
      she'd have you coming and going

when I wasn't around
did he go down there
      by himself
and get some?

he told me once
that an artist friend of his
spent an entire afternoon
explaining to him
that the whole universe
revolves around
a woman's ass

he also told me
he wanted to be
reincarnated
as a female bicycle seat

my father
the spiritual philosopher.

FLASHDANCE (1983)

My first silver screen erection

twelve years old
an aching boner
battling the fabric of my jeans
to get some air

my mother sat beside me
she took me to see
Jennifer Beals' gyrating thighs
her glistening ass
(or at least Jennifer's body double's)

what would Freud say?

when actual scenes of nudity
        came on
        strippers dancing for men and money
        my mother covered my eyes
        and said, "Oh, you shouldn't be watching this"
        but her voice was laughter-light

I slapped her hand away
and my cock pulsed and quivered
a rooster tied in a sack

maybe this is why I have always loved
dark haired women?

WARGAMES (1983)

I hold my son's hand
as we walk by the three unit
apartment house
that I used to live in
with my mother

we are walking to the Rideau Canal
only a block away
to go skating

fade to me
and my mother
lacing up

our nightly ritual
of skating
and hot chocolate rewards

coming back home
switching on my
Commodore 64
to work on coding
my video game
doing my best Matthew Broderick
impression

how much did I worry
about mushroom clouds
or computers going ape?

it wouldn't be until next year
that Cameron would give us Skynet
and a year after that
in which
Sting would dream of blue turtles

I Schwarzenegger time travel
through my mind

fade back to me
lacing up my son's skates
my daughter racing ahead

what will they worry about?
environmental disasters?
global epidemics?
will there even be a canal to skate on?

I push the thoughts away
focus on the hot chocolate ritual

important meanings
taught to me
by my mother.

THE MAN WITH TWO BRAINS (1983)

The Mayfair theatre was packed
    it felt like hide–and–seek
    with your cousins
    hiding in your grandma's closet
    full of heavy coats

Steve Martin double billed with The Jerk
the audience roared and howled
like they all had their filters cleaned

I was there with my new step family
my father remarried a lady from Toronto
she had three kids close to my age

she was a big lady
like my father had become
John Candy FAT
    I met her and her brood
    for the first time
    only a week before
    she and my father got hitched

it was during the Christmas holidays
she had a big gingerbread house
on her dining room table

she told me to smash it
because I came from a broken home
then she roared and howled
her filter gone

she would crack eggs on my father's head
to test his patience

my mother and I
in our new apartment
only a ten minute walk to the Mayfair
dating the doctor
        living upstairs

my father
        happy again

my mother
        happy again

laughter was back in my life

I was a boy with two homes

Steve Martin reigned King.

POLICE ACADEMY (1984)

My brother and I
quickly spliced our DNA

my weekend visits
to see my father
turned into weekend vacations
to hang with my stepbrother

my stepmother sold corporate office furniture

we all lived above
my father's art gallery
in the giant retail space
open concept
            living in cubicles
            (groomed from young ages
                        for upper management)

we would gather
for Saturday night meetings
The Love Boat
            and Fantasy Island
Sunday morning Atari
brainstorming marathons

music hugged the air
above our heads
the soundtrack to my life
my father's reel to reel
blasting
            Howard Jones
            The Everly Brothers
            Men at Work

and he would sing along
with his opera voice
        the man just lacked wings
        his lungs blowing hallelujah
        my innocent embarrassed skin
        my astonished awe goose bumps

and our summer days
        scheduled by the start times
        in the newspaper ads
movies
        were what we did
every weekend
before we discovered
beer and weed and girls

we fancied ourselves
quite the critics
raving about lack of plot
sneering at lousy dialogue

with discerning eyes we watched
all the Police Academy films
and berated the incoherence of Dune
the banality of Oh, God! You Devil
        astutely declaring George Burns wasn't funny

we were Abbott and Costello
we were Siskel and Ebert
we were young and foolish

not a care in the world

68

and soon it would be time for the changeover

look for the flash in the upper corner
of your life

the reel of childhood
winding down

projector one
running out
of
tape

changeover

projector two
kicks on

tape one finishes
the reel spinning wildly
like the end of bathwater
hurtling down the drain

transition seamless.

TAKE THREE

Ran (1985)

There is a scene
in Kurosawa's masterpiece
a shot of horses galloping by
warriors perched atop

slow motion
a long mise-en-scène shot
an eternity for some
            waiting for the clowns
                    in front
                    to keep it down

some might cry art
            (Skittles snobs sobs)
others might cry pretentious
            (terrible Toblerone tears)

I was with my father
and stepbrother
and our laughter was raw
                    unstoppable

my father ran a serious art gallery
for serious artists
for serious collectors
            and here he was
            behaving
like an immature fourteen year old boy

and the Professor and Mary-Ann
            behind us
                    "Please, please, please,
                            please be quiet!"

the usher finally threatening eviction

the same thing had happened before
when I was even younger
      The Black Stallion
            had my father rolling down the aisle
            with his artist friend
       (pretty sure the beer and whiskey played a role)

I like to think my father laughed
      at its pompous sensibility

maybe he just found horses funny?

maybe that's why
I still don't care much for westerns?

a horse walks into a bar
      I can hear my father snickering.

The Breakfast Club (1985)

My stepmother
                Miss Mary
            she wore that name
            like a superhero cape
she even had the equivalent
            to the Batmobile
 a vintage yellow Checker cab
                she drove around town
                protecting the innocent citizens
                from becoming too boring

she would throw parties
for office executives
send them a sock in the mail
            come find the other one

her grand piano aesthetic
her pinball machine taste
of Coke and Pepsi
circa 1955
                giant billboards with giant smiles
                to sell you shaving cream
                ice cream
                whipped cream
                from the living room walls

her style complimented my father's
love of Elvis
            and the Beach Boys

she commissioned an artist
to paint pictures of the Avenue Diner
    ketchup bottles
    vinegar bottles
    stood with authenticity
        real food of the people
    the line cook
        wrinkled and worn
    from ten thousand
        over easy eggs
        two hundred miles
        of sausage links
        and a mountain of bacon

and didn't we go there
every morning for breakfast
    the usual
    being prepared
    as soon as we walked in the door

those were the Happy Days
when everything was possible
everything hip and cool

this is when I took up
smoking

it wasn't peer pressure
it was Humphrey Bogart
and Cary Grant
and Burt Lancaster
    with all their movie
        shine
    smoke curling like the hands
    of a belly dancer

I would be
as cool
as Judd Nelson
as John Bender

my dialogue with the world
would always be
that much wittier
that much smarter
that much more intense
with a dart hanging from my lip

my stepmother hated smoking

pretty sure she loved me.

The Color of Money (1986)

My stepfather taught me to shoot stick
in a pool hall
atop a strip club
downtown
on Bank Street

we would
sometimes play billiards
to make us better 8-ball players

he taught me about backspin
and setting up the next shot
he taught me about the angles
getting position
            kissing off the rails

he would tell me stories
of when he was a young intern
in the U.S.
during the Detroit riots

he was the only white man
in a theatre of blacks
watching In the Heat of the Night
watching Sidney Poitier get slapped
across the face
watching as Sidney slapped that white man
right back
watching the audience erupt
thunderous applause
watching the rest of the film
            a tad nervous

he told me about the time
he let this big black patient
into the white doctor's lounge
my stepfather had asked him in
to play pool

my stepfather always wanted
to be challenged
he got dirty looks
from the other doctors
he didn't care
the pool games were grand

it was a few months later
when he was heading home
after a long shift
of sewing up shotgun wounds
when a group of black men
surrounded him

he could see it all
going south in a hurry
he visualized himself
role reversed on a stretcher

he was ready to hand over
his wallet
his wristwatch

he was ready to enter
the fetal position kick-a-thon
when one of the men said
Dr. Howell?

it was black Eddie Felson
        from the doctor's lounge

hey fellas, this cat's alright

my stepfather taught me a few things
he taught me the long game

kindness
        (bank it in the corner)
may one day
save
your
ass.

9 1/2 WEEKS (1986)

It was time to get laid
all my friends
had bedded girls

we had all measured
our cocks
swapped notes
I figured I was average

it was July
and I was working
as a dishwasher
down in the market

I smoked a joint
with the line cook
after my shift
then rode off
on my bicycle
to meet up
with my girl

she was going away
to the East coast
the next day
for the summer

this was my one shot
to finally join my peers
to finally say
I was a man
I got some pussy

armed with a box of condoms
me and my girl
waited for my stepbrother
to finish screwing his lady

we held hands
on the couch
waited like we had an appointment
with our lawyer

when it was our turn
we went in
undressed
she lay on the bed
stiff as a board

my cock
limp as a wet sock

I kissed her tits
her belly
my cock rose up
I reached for the condoms

frantically I tried to put it on
my cock grew sleepy
the dope I'd smoked
wasn't helping

back to kissing her tits
back to the box of condoms

she remained stoic
her excitement
          nonexistent

eventually I got my rubber on
eventually I wiggled my way in

it was painful for both of us
I didn't know what the hell
I was doing

I looked into her eyes
and said
let's forget this

the sun was the only thing
coming

coming
through the windows
illuminating my failure
so strong and hot
it melted the porn film
of my mind

Mickey Rourke and Kim Basinger
we were not

I think we tried to sleep
for a few hours

when it was time
I walked her home
kissed her goodbye

the relationship
over.

THE LOST BOYS (1987)

With James Dean smoking
on my bedroom wall
and Lauren Bacall giving me
her best *hey sailor* look
every time I opened
my high school locker

weren't we all that

with our dog eared copies
of Bukowski
          Brautigan
                    and Burroughs

did we all read The Electric Kool-Aid Acid Test?
how many hits does it take
for your friend to jump through a second floor window?

I grew out my hair
to look like John Paul Jones
and we would trade our theories
bubblegum perception cards
of reality

smoke this and think about that
doing the psychobabble quick draws
and game show inspections of truth
trying to earn the best supporting nomination
for a drama

instead of the fat light bulb
over our heads
we replaced it with a black light
and watched the shadow people
dance against the walls

conversations with a tree stump
ninjas sitting on all the rooftops
worms and maggots crawling through
the asphalt street

weren't we all that
cutting edge thinkers
with a blonde or brunette on our shoulders
watching the Canada Day fireworks
on Parliament Hill

how many times
did the cops come
and ruin all the fun?

how many times did we
watch the ground bubble and froth
as those bloody pigs
poured out
our beer?

WITHNAIL & I (1987)

This is the film
that taught us to drink
like alcoholics

we memorized
Bruce Robinson's dialogue
watched a dozen times
as Richard E. Grant
demanded to have booze
demanded to have tea and cake

and didn't we laugh
and laugh
and keep mixing
rum and Coke after
rum and Coke

didn't we create
our own Rum Diary
that summer

The Doors played the intro
The Stones the melody
The Beatles shutting it down

didn't we recreate
the last days of 1969
on our porch
as we watched
            melancholy
            half drunk
the rain falling
on the other side
of the street

what were we going to do
with the rest of our lives
everything holding
so much weight
so much meaning

possibilities
as many as
raindrops in the sky.

Frantic (1988)

Nothing seemed to be happening
but somehow Harrison Ford knew
something was off
something wasn't right

my mother finally re-married
the doctor upstairs
       we celebrated with Indian food
       took photographs
       at the Experimental Farm

we moved into
a new house
with a pool

the water crystal clear

over at my father's
everyone was moving
too fast
everyone slightly out of focus

once again
       money
quickly becoming
       the horror sequel
       of my life

quarrels over expansion

the sweat on the brow
the Statue of Liberty
slipping of the edge of a rooftop

could he hold on?
would it slip o
                ff?
                would we get the Hollywood
                                        ending?

what would Hitchcock do?

step on your knuckles
slowly.

Dead Ringers (1988)

There was a bar in the Glebe
called the Five Fifteen

we would go there
with our fake IDs
to drink beer
listen to jazz

it was there
that we would often
run into this guy
a Carleton student
who studied philosophy

he would engage us
get us into discussions
about Zeno's paradoxes
move us into conversations
about the existence of God
about identity

during one debate
about solipsism
my other friend suggested
if he were to beat me
so severely
bringing me to the teetering point
of life and death
that I would know
that I would want so much
to believe in the existence
of another
to explain what was happening
that it couldn't be just my mind
it would be all the proof I would need

I said

>I might want to believe
>I may even actually believe
>but it doesn't make it true
>it's not proof of the existence of others

the philosophy student agreed

my friend looked like
he really wanted to hit me

after months of chit chat
we discovered
the philosophy student
was an identical twin

I asked him if he'd seen
Dead Ringers

he said it was the scariest film
he had ever seen

it was only about a year or so after
that the owners of the bar
managed to snort the whole thing
up their noses

I never saw the student
after the bar closed

nor the guy who looked just like him.

CHRISTMAS VACATION (1989)

It had become my tradition
Christmas Eve spent with my mother
her family
my Danish side

a towering marzipan cake
anointed with toothpick flags
always sat in the corner
of my grandmother's dining room

she made enough food
to put baby Jesus on Weight Watchers
enough Danish Aquavit slouched about
to put the Three Wise Men
under the table

then the late night drop off
at my father's
ready for the 5AM start
breakfast at the Chateau Laurier
before hitting the road
boogie woogieing all the way
to Toronto
where my step grandmother
had prepared turkey Armageddon

my stomach would do
the Ali rope-a-dope
bouncing back
in the eighth
to kill the dessert

my father
with his oval physique
would consume everything
with Chevy Chase enthusiasm

the only thing
the only food
he didn't like
was lemon meringue pie

my stepmother
had told her mother
that my father's
favourite thing to eat
in the whole wide world
was lemon meringue pie

and every time we would arrive
my step grandmother
would greet us
announcing to my father
         Oh, Jim, I've made your favourite

my father would smile politely

my stepmother would suppress a giggle.

Dad (1989)

My father
wasn't all hugs and kisses with
his father
or
his grandfather
          both hard men of the bible

my grandfather would beat my father
smack him good with a belt
lock him in the storage shed
doing God's work

my Canadian grandparents
went faithfully to church
every Sunday
went faithfully to Florida
every winter

I was about fifteen
when I went down to Florida
just me and my old man
to visit his folks

we went to church with them
(about the third time I'd ever been)
and I can't remember
what was so funny
but my father began to laugh
and this got me going
and by the end of the service
we both were near hysterical
          dirty looks were in abundance

my grandfather was
in the early stages
of Alzheimer's

at night he would kick and scream
about the German bombs
about World War II

we were coming back from the beach
walking up the stairs
to my grandparents' apartment
when we turned around
and there was grandpa
gone

we found him three hours later
he had been walking around
lost
the hot sun turning his shoulders
to candy cane red

only a few years later
we would visit my grandfather
in the hospital
the kind of place you only had to
            check in

he would lie in that hospital bed
sometimes he would scream
sometimes he would have his eyes closed
often they were open

he never said anything
I hated visiting
I always hoped for eyes closed

the nurses had placed tiny sponges
under each of his fingers
so he wouldn't dig his nails into
the palms of his balled fists

a lifetime of studying the Bible
a lifetime of praying to God
and this is what he got.

WHEN HARRY MET SALLY (1989)

Men and women can't be friends

I told my stepbrother
if you find me a girlfriend
give me a call

I was at my friend's apartment
coming off of mushrooms
when
the call came in

I've got a girlfriend for you
        he said
I'll be right over I told him

when I came home
there was my stepbrother
and his girl
and another girl
with dark hair
dipping towards short
with an underbite
but leaning towards pretty

I was charming and funny
being high and goofy

before she left that night
I kissed her
got her phone number

the next time
was her first time
and really mine too

it was slightly awkward
a little painful
but after that
it was all bondage and blowjobs
we became porn stars

she was Jewish
and her parents hated me
I was the bad boy with the long hair
and tight jeans

they didn't want their daughter
going out with the likes of me
a Gentile

she would pick me up in her parents'
station wagon
drive us out to the Experimental Farm
      we didn't leave until
      all the windows were steamed
      dripping with foggy sweat

the problem was
I wasn't in love

I told her about the problem
I told her I couldn't see her anymore
she said she wasn't in love either
she said she thought we were just having fun
I told her it wasn't going to work
that I needed to be in love

she cried and left

I saw her only once after that
ran into her at a bar
only said hello

I thought I saw her standing at a bus stop once
but I wasn't sure

the sex never got in the way

I should have remained her friend.

DESPERATE HOURS (1990)

Mickey Rourke's career was about to
take a hit below the belt
and Steve Martin was going all soft and cutesy
and my father and stepmother's empire
(which had grown
        into The Attack of the 50 foot Business)
        was being encircled by an army
                of angry bankers

my father and stepmother
had amassed such a ridiculous
Godfather: Part III fortune
        a five storey mill
        and an historic post office
        and an old fire station
        and stuffed all three with paintings
        and sculptures
        and modern art
        (even had a real gay artist working
                and living in one)

my stepmother had developed MS
and heart problems
and she had got herself a scooter
to get around her Andy Warhol like studio
and despite her ailing body
she continued her philanthropic ways
Thanksgiving always being a twenty-five person affair
a table the length of a fire truck
        hop on the scooter to pass the gravy

all these moments
       the mad joy of buying a full size carousel
       transporting it in your own truck
       travel here or there in one of our seven cars
       the crazy exuberance for art
                     for life
       made everything
       seem like we lived in a movie

yet all the moments between frames
       seemed so desperate
       the confusion and exhaustion
       that my stepmother wore
       like the Woman in the Iron Mask

the Frankenstein cables
       (the endless cans of Coca-Cola)
       hooking them up at 4AM
       to get the monster rolling again

my father took up smoking
       he sat a fat Humpty Dumpty
       in his office
       flicking ash
       and papers about
       making phone call
       after phone call

he was borrowing money
too busy for me
too busy for anything else
too busy to care about
       all the men with shirts and ties
       standing on the front lawn
       calling him out to play
       calling out his loans

my stepmother could see them
       did her best to run interference
       with all the king's horses
       with all the king's men

but the credits
were coming due
at the end
of this
motion picture.

PRETTY WOMAN (1990)

I met her first year
in my philosophy class

when she took off her clothes
in the daytime
in the sun
Plato and Aristotle cheered

her beauty matched
        my hunger for it
and how many sets did we play?
        always ending up
        40–love

she was the third woman I'd been with
the last I ever wanted

we lived on cigarettes and wine
        consumed each other
        the menu large
                the desserts ridiculous
                the up-down
                and do it again
        sweaty roll offs
        repeat

there wouldn't be a night after the first
that I didn't sleep with her

she would perform
Evel Knievel on my cock
almost breaking every bone
in my body

and a little later
she gave me VD

when the doctor
burned the warts off my cock
with his Mr. Freeze ray gun
each zap an incisor bite
made with Betty Page teeth

I still loved my girl
the whore.

WILD AT HEART (1990)

I was Sailor
      she was Lula
I was Henry
      she was June

every film I saw seemed to be
about sex
and love

I left my stepbrother
left my friends
moved in with my lover
right next door to my grandmother
      (I'm going to give Freud
           frequent flyer miles)

nobody was impressed with me
I didn't care
I would marry my girl
and live happily ever after

it would have made
a downright boring picture
if that had happened
now wouldn't it?

and of course
like predictable plot lines
it didn't.

THE FISHER KING (1991)

Robin Williams
as a homeless man
crazy from losing his family
yelling at imaginary
     demons in the sky

if you told me my father
would end up
     close to this
I would have said
     nobody would believe it
     I mean
     okay for a movie
     but that doesn't really happen

I was lying in my apartment
next to my girlfriend
when the phone rang

my stepsister
     crying
          hysterical
my stepmother had
     forgot her nitro pills to slip under
          her tongue
     when she felt her heart go

it was
one of the last things she had said to me
     I think your father is going crazy
     I agreed like she was saying it might rain
     she said
          no, really, I think he's lost his mind

I knew my father was   out there
       (his mania growing
       an enthusiastic ego with access to billboards
       neon signs and credit cards)
I just didn't know how far he   would   f
                                        a
                                        l
                                        l

when it all fell apart
for the second time.

TAKE FOUR

SLEEPING WITH THE ENEMY (1991)

It was right after Christmas
and I was still feeling
all so George Bailey

I'd travel to Toronto
to pick up my girl
at the train station

there were no
candy canes in her smile
it was Welcome to Pottersville

I couldn't get it out of her
until we got back home
to Ottawa

when I did
I ran off to my only friend
at the time
        I had deserted all the rest

I told him about
what she did
        sleeping with her ex

he told me tinsel and fairytales
he told me stardust and gumdrops
he told me a bunch of lies
        I wanted to hear

a month later she and he
went off to Toronto together
he was giving her a lift
to visit a girlfriend

when she came back
from her trip
she announced she was
moving out

she grabbed a few clothes
said she was going
to my friend's place
and left again

I ran over to his apartment
I tried to reason with her
this is when she told me
she hadn't been at her
girlfriend's place
she'd been with my friend
they spent the weekend
at the Four Seasons
            fucking

she went back up to his apartment
I stood outside in the snow
watching the huge fat flakes
falling around me

in Karate Kid style
I kicked the back window
of my friend's stupid Jeep
to my surprise and delight
it shattered

the police called me about it
I denied it
said he must be having bad luck

the next day I had lunch
with my father
told him what had happened

he did his best to console
my youthful devastation
but he was already wearing
his own
winter coat of sadness
too engrossed in his own
manic collapse
to really be helpful

and like out of a movie
driving home
we pulled up to a stop
at a traffic light
and in front of us
my friend and my girl
the cold winter wind
blowing at them
through the back window
of that stupid Jeep

I smiled

and like a good horror film
she came back
again and again
having to spend the rest
of that school year
sharing classes with her
every day
            having to disarm another bomb

one day soon after
she sat down in front of me
in my philosophy of religion class
and took off her coat

she had gotten a large blue tattoo
of an angel
on her back

how many times did I kiss
the flesh of that spot?

a bell rang
an angel got her wings.

UNFORGIVEN (1992)

Love Potion No. 9 turned out to be poison
it was The Crying Game for me
my heart Under Siege
booze keeping me Braindead

every moon was a Bitter Moon
every film was about The Lover
Poison Ivy and The Player

I dove head first
into a bottle
and stayed there
       a drunken Aladdin
       a pissed Dracula
       (kept the curtains shut tight)

my heart had made
Children of the Corn II: The Final Sacrifice

it was an Army of Darkness
it was Hellraiser III: Hell on Earth

the only thing that saved me
from my Heartbreak Ridge
was my friend
who introduced me to the films
of Clint Eastwood

I was The Rookie when it came to love
                to Where Eagles Dare

one film at a time
I crawled up the side of Coogan's Bluff
I crawled up The Eiger Sanction of my despair
and ran down The Gauntlet of my misery

one film at a time
my sorrow dried up
my eyes no longer wanted
to Play Misty for Me

my depression would eventually
          Escape from Alcatraz

I would no longer be The Beguiled
I was now one of Kelly's Heroes

Eastwood
          my Magnum Force

I got a new girlfriend
watched his latest
in a theatre in Toronto
while we shared a mickey of whiskey

did I feel lucky?

you bet I did, Punk

and my ex remained
Unforgiven.

BAD LIEUTENANT (1992)

Show me your ass

it was the summer of chicken
and porn

I ended up living with my father
and stepbrother
in a rented house in the Glebe
with a life size cement pink pig
to guard our lawn

they would test guide dogs
on our block
to see if they would bark
at the pig

I had one of the rooms in the attic
it was as hot as a wet cunt
up there

the house was a bit of a dump
my father was gone most of the time
he had found a new girlfriend
spent all his time at her place

I would come home
from my job with the NCC
            (the drudgery of splendor
            digging beautiful tulips
            planting beautiful marigolds
            weeding beautiful gardens
            by the beautiful canal)

to usually find my stepbrother
and my friends
watching my father's pornos
drinking beer
and cooking chicken

our glistening greasy chins
teeth pulling as the gristle snaps
away from the bone
her glistening ass
as she bellows out an orgasmic cry
as another fellow blows semen
across her belly
and tits

it was vile and disgusting
and we kept doing it
day after day

on a particularly hot day
breaking up the earth
in my garden of beauty
I asked my co-workers
       who really believed in God?

to my surprise
most put up their hands

I felt betrayed by their
blind faith
how could you believe in God
making eight bucks an hour?

I would often take the bus
to Toronto on weekends
to visit
my new girlfriend

she was an artist
went to the Ontario College of Art

she had a love of needles
            and pipes
I would tie her up
fuck her on acid

we'd drink at the skuzziest bars
in Toronto's Chinatown
in Kensington Market
in the hood

how did I find myself
in the basement of a crack house
with a switchblade in my pocket?

me and my girl
the only
tighty whities there
when the Boyz n the Hood
decided to show up

she had been filming
with a school video camera
for an art project

I told her to
put the fucking camera away
before they knifed us

later that summer
she told me she was sick
of being tied up
sick of me

I was so upset
I drank a bottle of tequila
      accidently put my head
      through a window
           pane

later that summer
she told me she was pregnant

I went with her and her mother
to the hospital
got the crack baby scraped out

our relationship
aborted.

FALLING DOWN (1993)

When you have lost
everything that you have ever cared about
everything that was important
that's when
you park your car in the middle of traffic
and walk away

my father was being hunted
by the demons in his mind
that would manifest themselves
as the man across the street
talking on his phone
sent there to kill him

everything became
Three Days of the Condor
All the President's Men
Invasion of the Body Snatchers

there were billions of dollars at stake
the fate of nations
possibly to be determined
by the outcome
of this twisted cat and mouse
game of cloak and daggers
that was being unleashed
upon my father

all the cameras
directed at him
the ones hidden in the trees
the one in that man's tie clip

he was now in his own movie
nobody there to yell "Cut!"

I moved back in with mother
and stepfather
my father moved to a farm
on the outskirts of Ottawa
like a demented cult leader
set up his last art gallery
set up his last stand

the people who owned the property
were good people
but my father's illness had grown
too out of control for even them
to handle

they had him committed
for the first time to a psychiatric hospital
kicked him off the farm

for the rest of his life
it would be halfway houses
and dingy apartments
trips to and from the hospital
        some voluntary
        most not

for the rest of his life
it would be little jars of pills
medication swallowed
        some voluntary
        most not

for the rest of his life
he fell down
never managed
to get
back up.

WITTGENSTEIN (1993)

Philosophy
the Greek translates to
    the love of wisdom

I was in love with a new girl
a fellow philosophy student
and we would debate everything
like we were in a Woody Allen film

we would watch smart European movies
at the Bytowne
heated exchanges
over semantics, art, and logic
often followed

hanging out her was good for me
my grades zigzagged
    up the charts
I actually began to care
about school
    (in 25 million years
    will anyone remember?
        stay away
        from the big picture
        focus your lens
        on making meanings
        in the here and now)

her own father had also been
mentally ill
before he died

I asked her once
walking to Chinatown
why she never talked
about her father

the question alone
brought her to tears

she didn't like to talk about him

can't say I blamed her.

Reality Bites (1994)

It was coming up
to Christmas vacation
my father was all holiday cozy
safely locked up
in the mental hospital

I had brought him a couple of cartons
of cigarettes to keep his locomotive mouth
rolling along

my essay on Hegel
was due the next day
if you aren't familiar with German philosophers
they make trigonometry
look like the Sunday funnies

and didn't I sneer at Ethan Hawke
sitting there reading Being and Time
what a Holden Caulfield phony
he was

I was cool with Kant
Schopenhauer
Nietzsche
but Hegel
fucking Hegel
I didn't understand what the hell
he was saying
I couldn't wrap my mind around it

in desperation
I called my girlfriend for help
she had already written her paper

I don't recall exactly what she said
it was encouraging
not too much though
in the way of nuts and bolts

I began to cry
      deep big sighing wails
      like a toddler who
      skinned his knee

I didn't want my mother
or my stepfather
to hear me
      I shut my bedroom door
      and hid under the blankets
      my failure too embarrassing
      my failure too painful
      to share with them

she talked me through it
like Burgess Meredith
talking to Stallone

I rallied like Rocky
sat up all night
worked the keys
pounded out the paper

it was such misery
the muscles in my back
felt like the shell of a walnut

I felt so stupid

the next day I raced to get the paper in on time
ended up dropping it at my professor's house
racing off to the airport

that afternoon
I sipped a Margarita at the poolside bar
in Mexico
like a villain in a Bond film
while I thought about my poor father
        eating peanut butter on toast
        from the silver trolley in the hallway
        drinking coffee out of Styrofoam cups

I got an A– on the paper

and to this day
I still don't understand
fucking Hegel.

JUDGE DREDD (1995)

It was a Death Race 2000 against the clock
in action hero style
    with the sweaty T-shirt of Die Hard
    and the wrinkled brow of Predator
my friend and I were
trying to make it
to the movies
on time

I was in Toronto
and it was such a beautiful
    sunny summer day
and there we were
doing our best Chariots of Fire
to sit in the dark

but then the script had us run into
a snag
a sea of people
blocking our way to the Uptown Theatre
    how many times have you seen
    the chase sequence
    cut through the parade?

they were coming
down Yonge Street
in leather assless chaps
cracking whips
like stars of an S&M video
and the Village People cops
and the dragonfly Queens
escorting Svend Robinson
escorting Mayor Hall
flying their rainbow flags
marching proud

we Dolph Lundgrened our way
through the cheering crowd

would we make it?
would we catch the previews?

cut to
two grown men
slightly out of breath
sitting beside one another
sharing a bag of popcorn
watching Stallone's well muscled frame
run around his dystopia in tight spandex

we celebrated Gay Pride
in our own way
that day.

Billy Madison (1995)

Attendance hinders progress
not performing up to potential
Chris needs to apply himself more

it was true
I never tried very hard
never wanted to

aside from spelling
and reading
school was always so easy
as pi
       the calculus
       of a gumdrop
       travelling the circumference of this
            piece of cake

I was undeserving
       sometimes I still feel that way
       how have I been so lucky?

I graduated from middle school
I graduated from high school
and now here I was
graduating from University
and I still felt
       I hadn't studied hard enough
       I hadn't cared enough
       I hadn't suffered enough

at the same time
I knew it wasn't true
I had worked hard
and I was hoping my father would come
see me graduate
make him a proud papa

he never showed up
then shortly after
I got a call
from somebody at the hospital

I rushed there
found him sitting on a bench

the big happy smile
of the rope burn around his neck
beginning to scab over

the beam had broken

I hugged him

he hugged me back

the new graduate.

FROM DUSK TILL DAWN (1996)

My Danish grandmother
got cancer and died
I broke up with my girlfriend
of four years
and my father
          armed with a bottle of pills
          failed to leave the earth
          once more

I spent the next two years at college
after university
studying computer programming
          many late nights
          far too many early mornings

I'm not really sure how
but I graduated again

got a job with the government
moved in with couple of friends
and turned into an alcoholic

my one good friend and I
spent the best part of the next year
floating in a pitcher of draft beer

we would both go to work
hungover
hating our jobs
hating the mere mortals of the world
hating ourselves

we would barely make it
through the day
then do it again
drink until our heads
turned into pumpkins
at midnight

we would rant and rave
about the world's injustice
about its beauty
about how everyone was missing it

at the end of the night
we'd eat shitty pizza
and collapse into our respective comas

Tap, Tap, Tap

"Pssssstttt, hey, Chris?"

it was dawn
I had to get up in an hour
put away my vampire costume
for the day

there was a zombie
throwing pebbles at my window
a different undead friend
who had been travelling down the hypodermic highway
all night long
       he was brilliant
       possibly manic depressive
       didn't trust him around loose change
       and I was honoured to call him
       my friend

From Dusk Till Dawn
he'd been doing speedballs

he wanted to borrow bus change
he wanted to crash in my bed
for a tasty hour
before going to work

I got up
let him in the side door
took a shower
left him some money
and went to work

my Trainspotting buddy
would begin to turn his life around
in a few short years
but testicular cancer
would kill him shortly after that

and my Barfly pal
well he almost became a priest

I don't see his reflection anymore

and me
            the bats have been locked in the belfry
I love myself with the zeal of a self motivational tape
try to cook often with garlic
still hate my job.

AFFLICTION (1997)

My father hardly ever drank
I saw him drunk once
at his buddy's house
in Toronto
a guy he used to play in a band with
before he dropped out of university

my stepfather was a functional alcoholic
after a bottle of wine at dinner
he and I would go down to the pub
almost every night when I was
finishing university
we would sit and talk
smoke cigarettes
discuss the world
discuss Hemingway
            he loved Hemingway
            wanted to be just like him

after two or three pints
we'd stumble home
crack another bottle
            or drain back some whiskey
            that tasted like pornography

I got a call from my mother
said that my stepfather had been pissing blood

they diagnosed him with bladder cancer

the good doctors took it out
replaced the bladder with a hole
in the side of his abdomen
stuck an ostomy bag over it
to collect his urine

after the surgery
he would still go by himself
across the street
to the pub

afflicted.

TITANIC (1997)

My friend showed me a picture of her
it was a high school graduation head shot
she looked like Drew Barrymore
       with dark hair
I thought she was Italian

my friend said
I just had to meet her
that we would be Bogart and Bacall
       William Powell and Myrna Loy
       Fred Astaire and Ginger Rogers
       we would be great together

it was a set up
on her maiden voyage
from Edmonton
to Quebec City to do her Masters
at Laval University

she lived in a dump of a place
but she had a small TV
and a VCR with get-up-and-go
and I would go visit her
with a stack of rented movies

we would watch them
between making love
between the beer and the poutine
between the long walks
       around the old city

we had movie magic

she resurrected my heart
brought it back like Alien 4

the friend who had set us up
came with me one time
for Carnival
        she found us
        all so maple sugary sweet
        didn't know if she could stand it
        thought she might hurl

we dated long distance
for two years
before she came to live with me

nothing on earth
could come between us

she was Winslet
        I was DiCaprio

we were a Best Picture.

GOOD WILL HUNTING (1997)

Oh how I could relate
  math genius
  with issues
  fool friends
  loud and loyal
  drunk half the time

I could always find the straight lines
  find the numbers
  find the angles
  in the haze of a hangover
my Canadian grandfather
had taught high school math
  the calculations were in my blood

it wasn't just Will Hunting's story
that made me eat this film
  made me buy a VHS copy
  made me watch it a dozen times

it was Affleck and Damon
two young lads
who worked so hard
on a script
it landed them an Oscar
for Best Original Screenplay
won Robin Williams Best Supporting

if they could do it
maybe I could too?

I took out my pen
started to write

I've been doing it ever since

how do you like them apples?

THE TRUMAN SHOW (1998)

Imagine if you were the lead
in a production you weren't aware of
that you didn't know existed

you are the star
and the whole world is watching
you

you
and everything around you
and everyone around you
working for
you

imagine if it were true

my phone ringing
at my desk
at my government job
my father on the other end
telling me
about the millions
        of dollars
I would receive
that it was going to be great
his master plan
was going into effect

me telling him
      great
             please stop calling

RING RING, RING RING, RING RING

I had to be the first one
didn't I understand
it had to be me
I had to be the first one
it's part of the *plan*

my boss was giving me a funny look
because I'm on the phone *again*

RING RING, RING RING, RING RING

no dad
        really
                I can't
                    I'm at work

RING RING, RING RING, RING RING

I listened to him
his voice rising up
speaking even faster
speckled with a dash of anger
I was ruining the plan
I needed to come down
and receive the millions of dollars
that I was entitled to
for being the first one
to kick off his project

RING RING, RING RING, RING RING

please stop calling

RING RING, RING RING, RING RING

I'm sorry boss
       but I have to go
              and have my father
                    committed
                         again

RING RING, RING RING, RING RING

I went to the court house
swore on a bible
that my father was crazy

I went to the police
rode in the back of the cruiser
to pick him up

the officer asked me if there were any
guns in the house
I told him
the guys my father was living with
were hunters
so likely yes

the cop got backup
a female officer met us
at my father's

he went quietly

about an hour after I left the hospital
I got a call from my father
they had let him go

it was
back to the court house
back to the police
back to pick him up
back to the hospital

this time I stayed
pleaded with the doctors
said he had tried to kill himself before
said he needed help

they agreed to keep him

as I was leaving the hospital
for the second time that day
I heard over the PA
        "Code Blue to Emergency"
I saw three big orderlies run by me
I knew it was my father

I kept walking
didn't want to see that picture.

GIRL, INTERRUPTED (1999)

The doctors would get him
pretty doped up at times

we sat in a Chinese restaurant
on Somerset Street
across from the movie theatre
where we had watched
many films together

his brown nicotine stained fingers
like leather
sunsetting to honey yellow
closer to the knuckles
reaching for his pack
of Export A greens

my father had developed
small tremors
his hands would shake
as he brought his cigarette
to his lips

his eyes looked bulbous and dull
like fat grapes with the skins removed
his movements animatronic

he wouldn't speak
            much
he would just smoke
            and smoke
            and smoke

I called his doctors
got them to tone down
the android medication

we would meet for lunch
or dinner
once a week

I can't say I enjoyed
these visits

I went out of
a sense of
duty

a fragmented relationship
an old film
that has been spliced together
too many times
the picture popping and twitching
so grainy
                you almost wouldn't recognize him
                                anymore

one day
his eyes wet
he said to me
                it's supposed to be
                the other way around
                I'm supposed to be
                looking after you
I told him it was okay
life is unpredictable

the theatre
on Somerset Street was
demolished
the next year
making room for a supermarket
and parking lot.

THE SIXTH SENSE (1999)

I never saw the ending coming
that was the brilliance of the thing

it was Father's day
and my girlfriend and I
          (who would one day be my wife)
were waiting with spaghetti and meatballs
          wearing obligation like an itchy sweater
          getting prepared to gurgle and spit small talk
          ashtrays at the ready

I told him to make sure to take a shower
before he comes over next time
          (this to my father
                    always so Colgate fresh
                    tie tied tight
                    shirt freshly laundered
                    ironed out by math)

my girlfriend poked and prodded my reluctance
when he didn't show up
late by an hour

and off we went
on that warm summer day

and then
the ambulance outside
his shitty apartment

Bruce Willis sees the wedding ring fall
and with it
          the clarity of 6000 lumens

I see a dead person
my father lying on his bed
surrounded by his last few remaining
pieces of art from his fallen empire

I pull off his ring
and gold chain from his wrist

he never saw this ending coming
his brilliance gone.

FINDING FORRESTER (2000)

If you put it in a movie
nobody would believe it

my stepfather was a brilliant man
he reminded me of Sean Connery
in his role of William Forrester
wry, extraordinarily smart

the year my father died
my stepfather told my mother
it could be him next year

his cancer was on the move

the year my father died
I received an honorable mention
in the city's library writing contest

I was determined
next year
to do better
make my stepfather proud

he had always wanted to be
a writer like Frederick Exley
the drinking was never a problem

he couldn't write the word
"fuck"
while his parents were alive

I wrote "fuck" in my new short story
and the next time around
won 500 bucks
and first place
he came to see me get my prize
although I don't even know if he actually
got to see me collect
his piss bag had begun to leak
he had to dash out

I got a call from my mother
early in the morning
on the anniversary of my father's
death
she was going to the hospital
said there were only hours
left

a few hours later
she called again
said my stepfather couldn't speak
said she was going to put
the phone up to his ear
so I could say goodbye

I always
had trouble saying "I love you"
we didn't have that kind of relationship
he didn't say it either
but I knew he did

when she put the phone
up to his ear
I said "catch you next time"
I said "see you on the flip side"
I said "I love you"
          but I don't if he heard me
          did she pull the phone away
          too quickly?
it didn't mater
he already knew

my stepfather died
on the same day
as my father
exactly one year later

if you put it in a movie
nobody would believe it.

Take Five

PEARL HARBOR (2001)

The sneak attack

don't we all live
our lives in pictures

and didn't these burn
acid scars
on our collective unconsciousness
            the new Kennedy assassination
            where were you when it happened?
            what were you doing?

my father-in-law was sitting with his wife
on the tarmac of the Ottawa airport
ready to take off
when the call came in
for the plane
to turn around and go back
to the gate

when the first one hit
I didn't think anything of it
thought it might have been
a small plane

an accident

I was at work
went for a coffee break

I came back and told my
wife-to-be to turn on the TV

when the second one hit
we all knew

black tire tracks that veered
off
into the sky

it was my friend's birthday
that day
and he came over with some others
and we gathered around
to watch the pictures on CNN

I was so Tinsel Town cynical
I remember saying
I bet they'll make a movie
with Nic Cage
about this
there'll be a shot of him
running down the stairs
in slow motion

it would only take
five years
for Oliver Stone
to give it to me

it changed the world
how we do business
cost us wars
too many lives

Hollywood stayed pretty
much the same

I'll never forget
        my friend's birthday.

8 MILE (2002)

Cut to me
practically married
riding the bus to work
riding the bus to my office job
hung-over

I'd sit in meetings
where people actually got excited
over the appearance of doughnuts

fuck my wife
watch TV
go to work
eat a doughnut

this couldn't really be my life?
this couldn't be my next 25 years
could it?

we were visiting my friends in Toronto
the ladies went off to see
Noam Chomsky
we ran off to see 8 Mile

it reminded me of Rocky
my affinity for the underdog
a tight black knit cap
        squeezing my brain

I made a renewed commitment
to become a writer

I would set the alarm for 5AM
to get up and write for an hour
before I had to begin the real day

some days were too hard
I'd hit the snooze bar
but then I'd lie there
thinking
       do you want to be a writer
       or do you just want to be
       another asshole who didn't try?

with that thought swirling in my head
like a pack of flying monkeys
up I would get
       angry with myself
       angry with the world
       angry like Marshall Mathers
vowing
one day I'll write something good

vowing
one day I'll write my way out.

THE RING (2002)

We would have gotten married
much earlier
if my wife had just agreed

I wanted Frankenstein
and The Bride of Frankenstein
I wanted a Corpse Bride
I wanted to get married
            on Halloween

I kept trying to sell her on it
Let's Make a Deal conversations
            imagine everyone in costume
            wouldn't it be fun?

she wanted a winter wedding
snowflakes and Christmas trees
pretty as freshly fallen snow

and The Ring she wanted
a thick silver band
with a glass stone
            hand crafted
            only worth
            a couple of hundred dollars

The Ring
            just one of the reasons I loved her
            she wasn't into the flash
            she wasn't about the spotlight
            she wasn't like a lot of women

The Ring was simple
                        pure
                        clean

we got married on the darkest night of the year
the winter solstice

it was beautiful
just like her.

KILL BILL: VOL. 1 (2003)

Spent most of this year
        and much of the previous
trying to impregnate The Bride

my sperm were like
all those ninja Kato look-a-likes
trying to stab Uma Thurman

they couldn't do it

it was an epic battle
twelve days
of every month
month after month

there was Kung-Fu sex
lie there in a coma sex
Japanese anime sex
black and white sex
colour sex

we couldn't conceive

I drove the Pussy Wagon
long and far
night after night
ended up in Asia

we began the adoption process
to get a little girl
from China

my girl finally got sliced open
surgery with a Hanzo blade
we were trying again

I did my best Richard Roundtree
        she did her best Pam Grier

we made sweet sweet love

and then suddenly
quick as a Black Mamba strike
we were expecting.

Spider-Man 2 (2004)

"I have to go to the bathroom,"
groaned my wife
pushing up on the arms
of the armrest
>   the suction of a bowling ball
>   being pulled from its leather case

it was opening day
the day my daughter was to be born
I was hoping we would make it
that she would hang on
before reality would smash threw the vault
and steal all the hours in the day

it had taken us almost three years
to conceive

my wife had suggested we make
a coffee table book of all the people
who had seen her vagina
>   Dr. Doom
>   Dr. Octopus
>   and Dr. Strange

we had no luck getting pregnant
until we went to Professor X
>   he wielded his powers
>   ran the tests
>   got the chemicals bubbling
>>   all mad scientist
>>   beakers and test tubes
>>   steaming dry ice

my daughter slow as usual
showed up
ten days late

I was Jor-El
        my universe before me
        tears ran down my face

my mother came in
to the hospital room
snapped my picture
        me holding my daughter
        a swathed white bundle
        me looking almost exactly
        like my father looked
        when I was born

my smile
        as big as The Hulk
gravity gone
        radiation high

I was soaring
        red cape
                fluttering
                in the wind.

THE AMITYVILLE HORROR (2005)

We bought a house
        bought a minivan

we used to own a condo
which was located next to a 7–11
behind busy Rideau Street
        it was all ambulances
        and fire trucks

        it was all crazy people
        their brains saturated in chemicals
        desperately needing a burrito
        at 3AM
        their car stereos BLASTING
        Van Halen

        it was
        kids smoking dope under my window
        receiving rude figure gestures
        at the suggestion of relocating to the park

now it was all
        quiet
no cars
        crickets (maybe)

until
at 3AM
the wail of my daughter

me looking a perturbed Ryan Reynolds
swinging a
car seat
back and forth
and back and forth

re-plugging her soother

I see a fly on the windowsill
of my perfect new home

I kill it.

Children of Men (2006)

My son had to be cut out
he weighed more than eleven pounds

when my daughter was a baby
it was always Babette's Feast
it was always a Big Night
she could wolf down three jars
in one sitting
            warm up with mashed peas
            entree with sweet potato and chicken
            finish with blueberry pie

my son ate like The Machinist
I couldn't get a thing into him
all he wanted to do
was suck on my wife's tit

eleven months later
she was exhausted
at her wits' end

she came to me in tears
said she couldn't breastfeed him
anymore
she was going back to work
in less than a month
what was she going to do?

I told her
            leave it to me
I grabbed my son
and left for the day

when he was good and hungry that afternoon
I took him to a Lebanese restaurant
got him a chicken shawarma sandwich
he went all Animal House on it
      ripping it apart
      stuffing chicken and bread
      into his mouth
      devoured it like a drunken college student

he was his father's boy.

JUNO (2007)

There is Harrison Ford
passing a stripper
passing a phone sex operator
    with her leopard skin dress
    with her Pulp Fiction haircut
    with her truck driver style
        pin-up-girl tattoo
        smeared across her bicep

there is Harrison Ford
passing Diablo Cody
her golden statue
her Oscar
for Best Original Screenplay

I sent my manuscript
my book of short stories
to over thirty publishers

it took almost twelve months
to hear back

most were no
two said yes
I went with the best one

and there is me
almost two years
after sending off my writings
in the mail

there is me
looking at the box at my doorstep

I pick it up carefully
like Dr. Jones picking up
the holy grail
and take it to the kitchen
find a knife
and delicately
surgically
slice it along the spine
slice it down the tape
cutting it open
the cardboard ribs
springing up
like a reverse trap door

I peel them back
tear away the paper packaging

from the kid that couldn't spell
from the kid that couldn't read
from the kid who failed grade four
there is my book

it wasn't gold
it wasn't shiny
but aside from the birth of my kids
it was the proudest day of my life

don't we all love
a Hollywood ending?

SYNECDOCHE, NEW YORK (2008)

Who would you
get to play you
in the movie
of your life?

who would you get to score the soundtrack?
who would direct?

recreating your life
with a map ratio of 1:1

the world is the stage
everything is part of the film

who better to play the part
than you?

it's always been about
choosing your roles carefully

you are what you pretend
you are

who would play your friends?
how many times have you played
that game with your friends?

wasn't your ego always so huge
thinking you're as big
as any celebrity
in the glossy rags
of the grocery store checkout rack
   the only difference being
   you hadn't been discovered
   yet

the Buddhist says
don't fool yourself
you're only as good as your last picture.

THE BLIND SIDE (2009)

What a ridiculous place
to get the call

we were on vacation
in Quebec City
sitting at some chain restaurant
a place
where the menu has big glossy pictures
of pasta
        burgers
                chicken fingers
a place
where crayons for children
are automatically drawn
when you walk in the door

my father-in-law had died

he'd been walking
with his personal trainer
when his heart gave out

I felt so bad for my wife
so bad that we had to be there
of all places
to receive such devastating news

my father-in-law
would ask me
if I'd written the bestseller yet
I'd assure him it was coming

I remember crying in the back
of the limousine
after having helped carry
his casket
to his grave

I was crying because I would
would never get to show him
I made it as a writer

all my fathers
gone.

INCEPTION (2010)

A man growing old
waiting in his mind

were the ideas planted in my childhood?
did I watch too many movies?
did we every answer the question
about solipsism?
how do I know all my memories
aren't just implants?
am I dreaming or awake?

I'm looking at the man in the mirror
watching him brush his teeth
noticing his hair is greying
thinning
edging towards
           patchy lawn

should it be shaved Full Metal Jacket?

his body going slightly Brando
needing to Rocky into shape

I've reached forty

           my intermission

so far
I've enjoyed all the characters
the script always fresh
full of twists and turns

there might a few scenes
that could be reshot
and definitely some could have been
cut
left on the editing room floor

have we figured out what genre
      this is?

leaning towards drama
giggling back to comedy

I spit into the sink
get dressed for work
go right back into the theatre

there are no guarantees
the tape won't break
or the power won't go out.
unexpectedly
but I'm definitely looking forward
to the second half

load my kids into the minivan
shut the doors
the interior lights fade out

pass the popcorn
the rest of the movie
is about to start.

THE TREE OF LIFE (2011)

Fade in

it's a warm sunny
autumn day
       the buttery yellow
       the toffee gold
       and the red liquorice leaves
       beneath our feet
       crunching away
       the theatre sounds of munching popcorn

my daughter is running ahead of me
my son
       (far too big and heavy)
riding on my shoulders

my wife is a few steps back
holding the leashes of our two dogs
       noses bigger than their brains
       inhaling the smells of the Gatineau Hills
       with the zeal of a child
       and the power of an industrial vacuum

and my mother with her
toaster oven
sized camera case
is bringing up the rear

she is now several years into retirement
she is now several years into doing what she loves
taking pictures

the trail we are walking
is where she comes
every week
to photograph
birds

she takes pictures
for the local paper
takes them of the mayor
takes them of the Royal Couple
takes them of the Stanley Cup

when she was a child in Denmark
she loved to watch American cowboy movies
and she fell in love
      with the Southern United States
      Hang 'em High country

she's been down there several times
      smuggled the whole country home
      in the guts of her camera

she's been Around the World in 80 Days and
      65 years
photographing the volcanoes of Iceland
the faces of Tunisia
the churches of Mexico
the Great Wall of China

but the thing I think
she treasures most
      taking pictures
      of her grandkids
      her family

stop by that tree for a picture
she says

we gather ourselves
heap together
squeeze tight
       do our best CHEESE

fabulous she says
as she snaps
the picture

I think I got a good one
she says

my mother
a lens like Leibovitz
a talent like Karsh

my heart swells with pride

fade out.

THE MUPPETS (2011)

In the dark
sharing it with strangers
sharing it with family
anticipating
the trailers

coming soon
to a theatre near you

all the comedies
all the horror movies
all the dramas

the rest of my life
the rest of yours
the rest of theirs

always hoping for the buttery combo
the fizzy soda
the chocolate covered almonds

always hoping for the
free refill
      Kermit the Frog
      reincarnated
            Jim Henson's DNA
            hurtling through space and time
            like a chicken shot from a cannon

my son tugs on my sleeve
"I have to go pee."
"Me too," says my daughter

"Okay, let's go. Hurry, we don't want to miss the previews."

my kids hold my hands
as we walk down the hallway
posters of pictures
forthcoming

I snapshot this moment
tuck it into my mental wallet

this picture worth it all.

CREDITS

This book is about my life and I wouldn't be here and wouldn't be the person I am without my parents: my father, Jim McPherson; my mother, Judith Gustafsson; my stepmother, Mary O'Neil; and my stepfather, Wayne Howell. Jim, Mary, and Wayne, R.I.P. Mom, please live to a hundred years old.

To the owners (past and present) of the Mayfair Theatre and the Bytowne Cinema, thank you. Without these two Ottawa impendent theatres, my life would be horribly different.

Ross Buskard, Jeffrey Hodgson, George Sneyd, Judith Gustafsson, Michael Dennis, and Nicole Hillmer, thank you all for reading early drafts and giving me feedback.

Thanks to all my friends, family and co-workers who keep supporting what I love to do.

A very special thanks to my publisher, Chris Needham. Word.

And finally my wife, Marty Carr and my kids, Molly and Henry. It's always about you, for you. My love always.